MOON-BELLS
and Other Poems

by

TED HUGHES

Illustrated by Felicity Roma Bowers

THE BODLEY HEAD

London

The illustrations reproduced within
Moon-Bells and Other Poems are monoprints.

British Library Cataloguing
in Publication Data
Hughes, Ted
Moon-Bells and other poems
I. Title   II. Bowers, Felicity Roma
821'.914   PR 6058 U37
ISBN 0-370-30762-3

Printed in Great Britain for
The Bodley Head Ltd
32 Bedford Square, London WC1B 3EL
by William Clowes Ltd, Beccles
First published by Chatto & Windus 1978
This edition, with three additional poems, 1986

Contents

PETS

A dark November night, late. The back door wide.
Beyond the doorway, the step off into space.
On the threshold, looking out,
With foxy-furry tail lifted, a kitten.
Somewhere out there, a badger, our lodger,
A stripe-faced rusher at cats, a grim savager,
Is crunching the bones and meat of a hare
Left out for her nightly emergence
From under the outhouses.

The kitten flirts his tail, arches his back –
All his hairs are inquisitive.
Dare he go for a pee?
Something is moving there, just in dark.
A prowling lump. A tabby tom. Grows.
And the battered master of the house
After a month at sea, comes through the doorway,

Recovered from his nearly fatal mauling,
Two probably three pounds heavier
Since that last time he dragged in for help.
He deigns to recognise me
With his criminal eyes, his deformed voice.
Then poises, head lowered, muscle-bound,
Like a bull for the judges,
A thick Devon bull,
Sniffing the celebration of sardines.

NESSIE

No, it is not an elephant or any such grasshopper.
It's shaped like a pop bottle with two huge eyes in the stopper.

But vast as a gasometer, unmanageably vast,
With wing-things like a whale for flying underwater fast.

It's me, me, me, the Monster of the Loch!
Would God I were a proper kind, a hippopot or croc!

Mislaid by the ages, I gloom here in the dark,
When I should be ruling Scotland from a throne in Regent's Park!

Once I was nobility – Diplodocus ruled the Isles!
Polyptychod came courting with his stunning ten-foot smiles.

Macroplat swore he'd carry me off before I was much older.
All his buddy-boys were by, grinning over his shoulder –

Leptoclid, Cryptocleidus, Triclid and Ichthyosteg –
Upstart Sauropterygs! But I took him down a peg –

I had a long bath in the Loch and waiting till I'd finished
He yawned himself to a fossil and his gang likewise diminished.

But now I can't come up for air without a load of trippers
Yelling: 'Look at the neck on it, and look at its hedge-clippers!

Oh no, that's its mouth.' Then I can't decently dive
Without them sighing: 'Imagine! If *that* thing were alive!

Why, we'd simply have to decamp, to Canada, and at the double!
It was luckily only a log, or the Loch-bed having a bubble.

It was something it was nothing why whatever could it be
The ballooning hideosity we thought we seemed to see?'

Because I am so ugly that it's just incredible!
The biggest bag of haggis Scotland cannot swallow or sell!

Me, me, me, the Monster of the Loch!
Scotland's ugliest daughter, seven tons of poppycock!

Living here in my black mud bed the life of a snittery newty,
And never a zoologist a-swooning for my beauty!

O where's the bonnie laddie, so bold and so free,
Will drum me up to London and proclaim my pedigree?

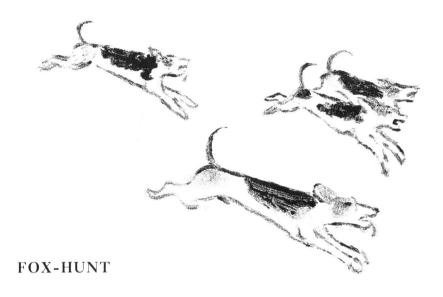

FOX-HUNT

Two days after Christmas, near noon, as I listen
The hounds behind the hill
Are changing ground, a cloud of excitements,
Their voices like rusty, reluctant
Rolling stock being shunted. The hunt
Has tripped over a fox
At the threshold of the village. A crow in the fir
Is inspecting his nesting site, and he expostulates
At the indecent din. A blackbird
Starts up its cat-alarm. The grey-cloud mugginess
Of the year in its pit trying to muster
Enough energy to start opening again
Roars distantly. Everything sodden. The fox
Is flying, taking his first lesson
From the idiot pack-noise, the puppyish whine-yelps
Curling up like hounds' tails, and the gruff military barkers:
A machine with only two products:
Dog-shit and dead foxes. Lorry engines
As usual modulating on the main street hill
Complicate the air, and the fox runs in a suburb
Of indifferent civilised noises. Now the yelpings
Enrich their brocade, thickening closer

In the maze of wind-currents. The orchards
And the hedges stand in coma. The pastures
Have got off so far lightly, are firm, cattle
Still nose hopefully, as if Spring might be here
Missing out winter. Big lambs
Are organising their gangs in gateways. The fox
Hangs his silver tongue in the world of noise
Over his spattering paws. Will he run
Till his muscles suddenly turn to iron,
Till blood froths his mouth as his lungs tatter,
Till his feet are raw blood-sticks and his tail
Trails thin as a rat's? Or will he
Make a mistake, jump the wrong way, jump right
Into the hound's mouth? As I write this down
He runs still fresh, with all his chances before him.

I SEE A BEAR

I see a bear
Growing out of a bulb in wet soil licks its black tip
With a pink tongue its little eyes
Open and see a present an enormous bulging mystery package
Over which it walks sniffing at seams
Digging at the wrapping overjoyed holding the joy off sniffing and scratching
Teasing itself with scrapings and lickings and the thought of it
And little sips of the ecstasy of it

O bear do not open your package
Sit on your backside and sunburn your belly
It is all there it has actually arrived
No matter how long you dawdle it cannot get away
Shamble about lazily laze there in the admiration of it
With all the insects it's attracted all going crazy
And those others the squirrel with its pop-eyed amazement
The deer with its pop-eyed incredulity
The weasel pop-eyed with envy and trickery
All going mad for a share wave them off laze
Yawn and grin let your heart thump happily
Warm your shining cheek fur in the morning sun

You have got it everything for nothing

A MOON-WITCH

A moon-witch is no joke.
She comes as a sort of smoke.
She wisps in through the keyhole and feels about
Like a spider's arm or a smoke-elephant's snout
Till she finds her victim.
He collapses like a balloon – she has sucked him
Empty in a flash. Her misty feeler
Blooms red as blood in water, then milkily paler –
And fades. And a hundred miles off
She disguises her burp with a laugh.

Also she has a kind of electronic
Rocket-homing trick – and that is chronic.
She steals the signature
Of whoever she wants to bewitch
And swallows it. Now wherever he might be
He sees her face, horrible with evil glee,
Hurtling at him like a rocket – WHOP!
People see him stop.

He staggers, he smooths his brow, he is astonished –
Whatever it was, it seems to have vanished.

He doesn't know what he's in for.
He's done for.

Only deep in sleep he dreams and groans
A pack of hyenas are fighting over his bones.

In a week, he dies. Then 'Goodness!' the witch says,
And yawns and falls asleep for about ten days –
Like a huge serpent that just ate
Something its own weight.

ROE-DEER

In the dawn-dirty light, in the biggest snow of the year
Two blue-dark deer stood in the road, alerted.

They had happened into my dimension
The moment I was arriving just there.

They planted their two or three years of secret deerhood
Clear on my snow-screen vision of the abnormal

And hesitated in the all-way disintegration
And stared at me. And so for some lasting seconds

I could think the deer were waiting for me
To remember the password and sign

That the curtain had blown aside for a moment
And there where the trees were no longer trees, nor the road a road

The deer had come for me.

Then they ducked through the hedge, and upright they rode their legs
Away downhill over a snow-lonely field

Towards the tree-dark – finally
Seeming to eddy and glide and fly away up

Into the boil of big flakes.
The snow took them and soon their nearby hoofprints as well

Revising its dawn inspiration
Back to the ordinary.

TIGRESS

She grin-lifts
Her black lips and white whiskers
As she yearns forward

Complaining
Tearing complaint off and banging it down a long pipe
That echoes and hums after

Her stride floats
Enjoying a weightlessness
A near-levitation

Again her cry
Scours out the drum of her

Her face
Works at its lacks and longings and quells
Its angers and rehearses its revenges
Endlessly

She lifts again
The welded and bolted plates of her head
Like an illness past curing

She rolls groaning
A bullet of anguish out of her

She is moving, in her hanging regalia
Everything in her is moving, slipping away forward
From the hindward-taper, drawing herself
Out of the air, like a tail out of water

A bow on the war-path, carrying itself
With its dazzling and painted arrows

Shoulders walling her chest, she goes
Between travelling armed walls

Lifting her brow as she walks to ripple
The surface of the element she moves in

Her cry rips the top off the air first
Then disembowels it

She lies down, as if she were lowering
A great snake into the ground

She rests her head on her forepaws, huge trouble
All her lines too enormous for her

I look into her almond eyes. She frowns
Them shut, the fur moving down on her brows.

MOON-WHALES

They plough through the moon-stuff
Just under the surface
Lifting the moon's skin
Like a muscle
But so slowly it seems like a lasting mountain
Breathing so rarely it seems like a volcano
Leaving a hole blasted in the moon's skin

Sometimes they plunge deep
Under the moon's plains
Making their magnetic way
Through the moon's interior metals
Sending the astronaut's instruments scatty

Their music is immense
Each note hundreds of years long
Each complete tune a moon-age

So they sing to each other unending songs
As unmoving they move their immovable masses

Their eyes closed ecstatic

THE MOORHEN

Might not notice you.
She's policing the water-bugs
In her municipal uniform.

A watchful clockwork
Jerks her head ahead, to inspect ahead
At each deep tread
Of her giant, ooze-treading claw-spread.

Her undertail flirts, jerk by jerk,
A chevron blaze, her functionary flash,
And the blood-orange badge or bleb
On her helmet neb
Lets the transgressing water-skeeter know
The arresting face, the stabbing body-blow
Is official.

Her legs are still primaeval,
Toy-grotesque
As when she – this thistledown, black, tiptoe –
Scootered across the picture-skin of water.

Lumpier now, she hurdle-strides into flight
Across stepping stones of slapped circles

Then dangles her drape of webs below her
Like a hawthorn fly, till she hoicks up
Clear over the bull-rush plumes, and crash-drops

Into her off-duty nervous collapse.

COMING DOWN THROUGH SOMERSET

I flash-glimpsed in the headlights – the high moment
Of driving through England – a killed badger
Sprawled with helpless legs. Yet again
Manoeuvred lane-ends, retracked, waited
Out of decency for headlights to die,
Lifted by one warm hind leg in the world-night
A slain badger. August dust-heat. Beautiful,
Beautiful, warm, secret beast. Bedded him
Passenger, bleeding from the nose. Brought him close
Into my life. Now he lies on the beam
Torn from a great building. Beam waiting two years
To be built into new building. Summer coat
Not worth skinning off him. His skeleton – for the future.
Fangs, handsome concealed. Flies, drumming,
Bejewel his transit. Heatwave ushers him hourly
Towards his underworlds. A grim day of flies
And sunbathing. Get rid of that badger.
A night of shrunk rivers, glowing pastures.
Sea-trout shouldering up through trickles. Then the sun again
Waking like a torn-out eye. How strangely
He stays on into the dawn – how quiet
The dark bear-claws, the long frost-tipped guard hairs!
Get rid of that badger today.
And already the flies
More passionate, bringing their friends. I don't want
To bury and waste him. Or skin him (it is too late).
Or hack off his head and boil it
To liberate his masterpiece skull. I want him
To stay as he is. Sooty gloss-throated,
With his perfect face. Paws so tired,
Power-body relegated. I want him
To stop time. His strength staying, bulky,
Blocking time. His rankness, his bristling wildness,

His thrillingly painted face.
A badger on my moment of life.
Not years ago, like the others, but now.
I stand
Watching his stillness, like an iron nail
Driven, flush to the head,
Into a yew post. Something
Has to stay.

AMULET

Inside the wolf's fang, the mountain of heather.
Inside the mountain of heather, the wolf's fur.
Inside the wolf's fur, the ragged forest.
Inside the ragged forest, the wolf's foot.
Inside the wolf's foot, the stony horizon.
Inside the stony horizon, the wolf's tongue.
Inside the wolf's tongue, the doe's tears.
Inside the doe's tears, the frozen swamp.
Inside the frozen swamp, the wolf's blood.
Inside the wolf's blood, the snow wind.
Inside the snow wind, the wolf's eye.
Inside the wolf's eye, the North star.
Inside the North star, the wolf's fang.

ANTS

Can an Ant love an Ant?
Can a scissor-face

Kiss a scissor-face?
Can an Ant smile? It can't.

Why all that going and coming?
They run, they wave their arms, they cry –

The Ant's nest is a Nunnery
Of Holy Madwomen.

They race out searching for God.
They race home: 'He's not there!'

And their mad heads nod, nod, nod,
And they stagger in despair,

Bicycling, weeping, trembling (once
To have lost your only hope and yet to

Still have just a chance
Is enough to know what they go through!)

And carrying such a sob
In a body that's

Nothing but hard little knots
Or a scalding blob

Of molten copper trickling
Through a burning house!

Love of God is fierce!

But the sun's yokel earth only yawns and scratches the tickling.

BIRTH OF RAINBOW

This morning blue vast clarity of March sky
But a blustery violence of air, and a soaked overnight
Newpainted look to the world. The wind coming
Off the snowed moor in the South, razorish,
Heavy-bladed and head-cutting, off snow-powdered ridges.
Flooded ruts shook. Hoof-puddles flashed. A daisy
Mud-plastered unmixed its head from the mud.
The black and white cow, on the highest crest of the round ridge,
Stood under the end of a rainbow.
Head down licking something, full in the painful wind
That the pouring haze of the rainbow ignored.
She was licking her gawky black calf
Collapsed wet-fresh from the womb, blinking his eyes
In the low morning dazzling washed sun.
Black, wet as a collie from a river, as she licked him,
Finding his smells, learning his particularity.
A flag of bloody tissue hung from her back end
Spreading and shining, pink-fleshed and raw, it flapped and coiled
In the unsparing wind. She positioned herself, uneasy
As we approached, nervous small footwork
On the hoof-ploughed drowned sod of the ruined field.
She made uneasy low noises, and her calf too
With its staring whites, mooed the full clear calf-note
Pure as woodwind, and tried to get up,
Tried to get its cantilever front legs
In operation, lifted its shoulders, hoisted to its knees,
Then hoisted its back end and lurched forward
On its knees and crumpling ankles, sliding in the mud
And collapsing plastered. She went on licking it.
She started eating the banner of thin raw flesh that
Spinnakered from her rear. We left her to it.
Blobbed antiseptic onto the sodden blood-dangle
Of his muddy birth-cord, and left her
Inspecting the new smell. The whole South West
Was black as nightfall.

Trailing squall-smokes hung over the moor leaning
And whitening towards us, then the world blurred
And disappeared in forty-five degree hail
And a gate-jerking blast. We got to cover.
Left to God the calf and its mother.

BULLFINCHES

A mournful note, a crying note,
A single tin-whistle half-note, insistent
Echoed by another
Slightly bluer with a brief distance,
In March, in the draughty, dripping orchard.

And again, and again – and the echo prompt.
Bullfinch is melancholy.

Bullfinch wants us to feel a cold air, a shivery sadness,
And to pity him in his need,
In the poverty start of the year, the hungry end,
Too early
In his Persian plum-plush wedding regalia
Above bleak, virginal daffodils.

He wants us to feel protective
At least for as long as it takes him
To strip every tree of its bud-blossom

To pack a summerful of apple-power
Under his flaming shirt.

MOON-WALKERS

After a bad night's sleeping
All night the full moon's glare seeping
Between your closed eyelids, and you tossing and turning
With dreams of heaven burning
And cellars smoking with mystery
And erupting and debouching monsters from prehistory,

You wake with a cracking headache and eyes
Like lumps of lead, and to your intense surprise
You see all over the ceiling giant foot-tracks
Which have nothing to do with the blotches and cracks.

Enormous foot-prints of the lizard sort
Give you gooseflesh and sink you deep in thought.

So you carefully get out of bed
Ready to see your foot enclosed in an alligator-type head,

But your house is quite empty, not even a newt in a cup,
Only these giant mud-splodge claw-foot prints all over
    the ceilings wherever you look up

And all over the walls and everywhere
Over the furniture and the linen and then your hair

Really stands on end as you realise every one
Of these tramplers must have weighed at least a ton,

Nevertheless they came out like the far stars noiseless
    and weightless in the night
And vanished at first light

As if it were only the light which keeps them hid —
Or as if they came out of your dreams and went back in
    there (which they probably did).

A MOUNTAIN LION

A mountain lion, her alarmed skulk
Fearing to peel her molten umber
From shadows —
                              Her forefeet
Go forward daringly, a venture, a theft in them
Stealing her body away after —

She weaves, her banner's soft prisoner,
In her element of silence, weaving silence
Like a dance, a living silence
Making herself invisible magical steps
Weaving a silence into all her limbs

She flows along, just inside the air
Every line eluding the eye. Hesitation
And moving beyond
And by hesitation. All her legs like
A magical multiplication of one leg
Look at any one, the others are doing the walking
And slender and pressing
Forward through silence, becoming silence
Ahead and leaving it behind, travelling
Like a sound-wave, arriving suddenly.
Ahead of herself, a swift stillness.

HE GETS UP IN DARK DAWN

To misted stillness.
First thrush splutters and chips at the thick light.
Suddenly the room leaps, blue-lit. Was it lightning?
Then the crumplings and the bamboo-splittings
In echoey heaven-corridors, of close thunder.

He listens for the rain and it starts.
Taptap on the roof. The birds too,
Gurgling and exercising their highest and their lowest
And all the twisting stairs from one to the other,
Singing in dark holds of young leaves and unopened blossoms,
Not knowing who lives in the house, or who has lived,
Or what year this is, or what century this is.

Through thick vapour swaddle
Violet lightning shakes its shutters
And thunder trundles its drums from the highest attic
Of heaven to the lowest, furthest basement.
He stands at the open door and cannot go fishing.

He sits hearing his kettle. Lightning again
Tosses the kitchen, the birds bustle their voices
Echoless, squibby-damp, but not daunted
Out in the nodding, dripping, flickering, blue garden.
The thunder splits and lets its domes collapse.
Ginger, his cat, tenses and rises listening
To the step by step approach of the thunder

As if ghosts were creaking all over the house.
His head sleeks very slender, with ears
That both want to prick listening and to flatten.
Thunder unloads its last stamping arrival

As the lights jump in and out – the sky is falling –
He flattens –

His master explains with quiet, meaningless words.

WATER

On moors where people get lost and die of air
On heights where the goat's stomach fails

In gorges where the toad lives on starlight
In deserts where the bone comes through the camel's nostril

On seas where the white bear gives up and dies of water
In depths where only the shark's tooth resists

At altitudes where eagles would explode
Through falls of air where men become bombs

At the Poles where zero is the sole hearth
Water is not lost, is snug, is at home –

Sometimes with its wife, stone –
An open-armed host, of poor cheer.

MOON-WIND

There is no wind on the moon at all
   Yet things get blown about.
In utter utter stillness
   Your candle shivers out.

In utter utter stillness
   A giant marquee
Booms and flounders past you
   Like a swan at sea.

In utter utter stillness
   While you stand in the street
A squall of hens and cabbages
   Knocks you off your feet.

In utter utter stillness
   While you stand agog
A tearing twisting sheet of pond
   Clouts you with a frog.

A camp of caravans suddenly
   Squawks and takes off.
A ferris wheel bounds along the skyline
   Like a somersaulting giraffe.

Roots and foundations, nails and screws,
   Nothing can hold fast,
Nothing can resist the moon's
   Dead-still blast.

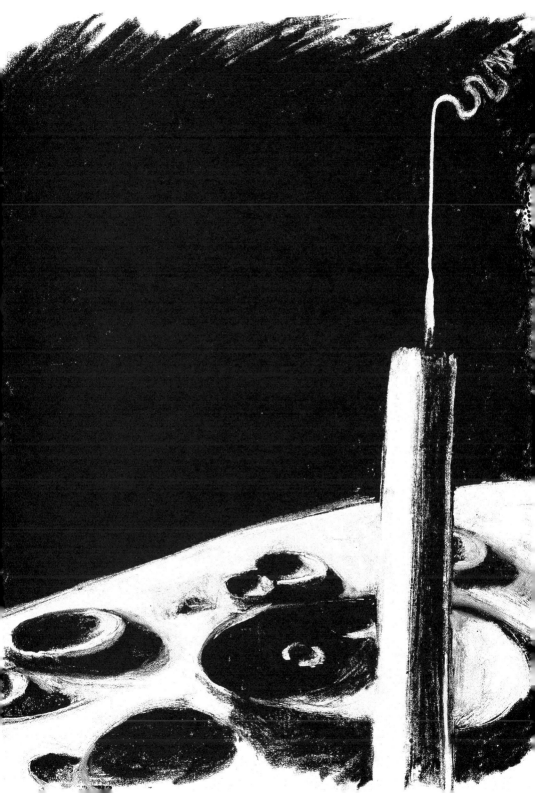

SKETCHING A THATCHER

Bird-bones is on the roof. Seventy eight
And still a ladder squirrel,
Three or four nitches at a time, up forty rungs,
Then crabbing out across the traverse,
Cock-crows of insulting banter, liberated
Into his old age, like a royal fool
But still tortured with energy. Thatching
Must be the sinless job. Weathered
Like a weathercock, face bright as a ploughshare,
Skinny forearms of steely cable, batting,
The reeds flush, crawling, cliff-hanging,
Lizard-silk of his lizard-skinny hands,
Hands never still, twist of body never still –
Bounds in for a cup of tea, 'Caught you all asleep!'
Markets all the gossip – cynical old goblin
Cackling with wicked joy. Bounds out –
Trips and goes full length, bounces back upright,
'Haven't got the weight to get hurt with!' Cheers
Every departure – 'Off for a drink?' and 'Off
To see his fancy woman again!' – leans from the sky,
Sun-burned-out pale eyes, eyes bleached
As old thatch, in the worn tool of his face,
In his haggard pants and his tired-out shirt –
They can't keep up with him. He just can't
Stop working. 'I don't want the money!' He'd
Prefer a few years. 'Have to sell the house to pay me!'
Alertness built into the bird-stare,
The hook of his nose, bill-hook of his face.
Suns have worn him, like an old sun-tool
Of the day-making, an old shoe-tongue
Of the travelling weathers, the hand-palm, ageless,
Or all winds on all roofs. He lams the roof
And the house quakes. Was everybody
Once like him? He's squirmed through
Some tight cranny of natural selection.
The nut-stick yealm-twist's got into his soul,

He didn't break. He's proof
As his crusty roofs. He ladder-dances
His blood light as spirit. His muscles
Must be clean as horn.
And the whole house
Is more pleased with itself, him on it,
Cresting it, and grooming it, and slapping it
Than if an eagle rested there. Sitting
Drinking his tea, he looks like a tatty old eagle,
And his yelping laugh of derision
Is just like a tatty old eagle's.

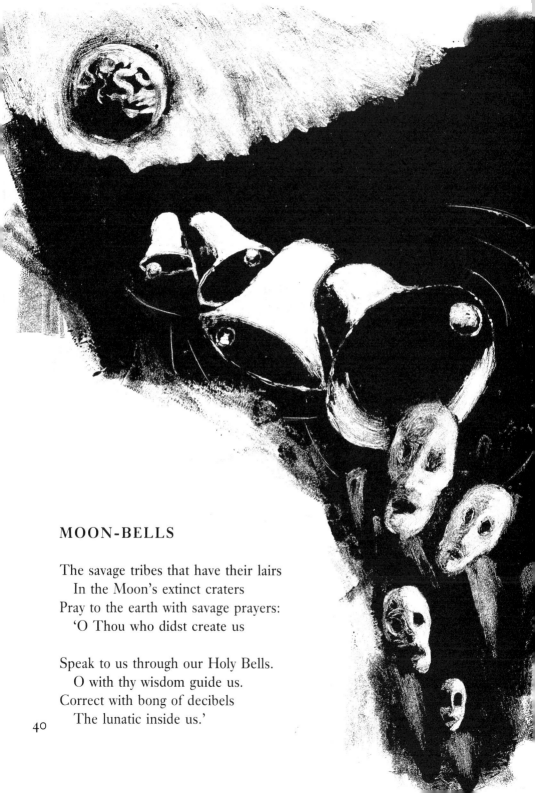

MOON-BELLS

The savage tribes that have their lairs
  In the Moon's extinct craters
Pray to the earth with savage prayers:
  'O Thou who didst create us

Speak to us through our Holy Bells.
  O with thy wisdom guide us.
Correct with bong of decibels
  The lunatic inside us.'

40

So then they swing the bells they have slung
   In each volcano's womb,
And earth begins to declare with clung
   And clang and mumbling boom

Out of one bell: 'Towers fall
   And dunghills rise.' And from another:
'He who thinks he knows it all
   Marries his own mother.'

'Only an owl knows the worth of an owl,'
   Clanks one with a clunk.
'Let every man,' groans one in toil,
   'Skin his own skunk.'

'The head is older than the book,'
   Shrills one with sour tone,
And 'Beauty is only skin deep
   But ugly goes to the bone.'

Then: 'He who does not swell in the warm
   Will not shrink in the cold.'
Another is muttering: 'Hair by hair
   You may pluck a tiger bald.'

'Going to ruin is silent work,'
   One dins with numbing bellow.
And: 'Love and Thirst, they know no shame,
   But the Itch beats them hollow.'

'All things, save love and music,
   Shall perish,' another cries.
'Downcast is King of Illness.'
   'Dead fathers have huge eyes.'

So on and on the bells declare
The Word of Earth to them up there.

MOON-RAVENS

Are silver white
Like the moonlight
And their croak, their bark
Is not dark
And ominous,
But luminous
And a sweet chime
Always announcing time
For good news to come
If there is some,
And if there isn't
Then there's a moon-present –
That is, a stillness,
And if you have any illness
It flits out of your mouth
In the shape of a black moth

Which the moon-raven then follows
And swallows.

HORRIBLE SONG

The Crow is a wicked creature
  Crooked in every feature.
Beware, beware of the Crow!
When the bombs burst, he laughs, he shouts;
When guns go off, he roundabouts;
When the limbs start to fly and the blood starts to flow
  Ho Ho Ho
  He sings the Song of the Crow.

The Crow is a sudden creature
  Thievish in every feature.
Beware, beware of the Crow!
When the sweating farmers sleep
He levers the jewels from the heads of their sheep.
Die in a ditch, your own will go,
  Ho Ho Ho
  While he sings the Song of the Crow.

The Crow is a subtle creature
  Cunning in every feature.
Beware, beware of the Crow!
When sick folk tremble on their cots
He sucks their souls through the chimney pots,
They're dead and gone before they know,
  Ho Ho Ho
  And he sings the Song of the Crow.

The crow is a lusty creature
  Gleeful in every feature.
Beware, beware of the Crow!
If he can't get your liver, he'll find an old rat
Or highway hedgehog hammered flat,
Any old rubbish to make him grow,
  Ho Ho Ho
  While he sings the Song of the Crow.

The Crow is a hardy creature
    Fire-proof in every feature.
Beware, beware of the Crow!
When Mankind's blasted to kingdom come
The Crow will dance and hop and drum
And into an old thigh-bone he'll blow
    Ho Ho Ho
    Singing the Song of the Crow.

OFF-DAYS

In the lowest pit of the solstice, among sour conifers,
The reservoir looked reluctant.
Shrunk low, lying as if ill
Beneath its rusty harness of old waterlines.
Its only life — shivers of patience.

Man-made and officially ugly
Its bed is a desert of black, private depression.
A second whole day we have called for a pike.
Nothing volunteers for election.

If there is one last pike — one old mule,
One last patriot,
It starves, resolutely legless,
Hunger closed,
Habit hardening to total absence
In this grave of spontaneity.

Wind off the lake-face, unexpected blows
Bleak as a knuckle
Is the water's only peevish trick.

Only try to imagine our dredging lures
Resurrecting one jerk of life
In the eyeballs
Of mud.

For days somebody's dead herring has lain
Miserably visible,
Like a failed bribe.

Finish!
The pike here
Have been reabsorbed by the outcrop.

All jaws have resumed the Jurassic!

EARTH-MOON

Once upon a time there was a person
He was walking along
He met the full burning moon
Rolling slowly towards him
Crushing the stones and houses by the wayside.
He shut his eyes from the glare.
He drew his dagger
And stabbed and stabbed and stabbed.
The cry that quit the moon's wounds
Circled the earth.
The moon shrank, like a punctured airship,
Shrank, shrank, smaller, smaller,
Till it was nothing
But a silk handkerchief, torn,
And wet as with tears.
The person picked it up. He walked on
Into moonless night
Carrying this strange trophy.